Pagan Portals
Zen Druidry

Living a Natural Life,
with Full Awareness

Pagan Portals
Zen Druidry

Living a Natural Life,
with Full Awareness

Joanna van der Hoeven

MOON
BOOKS

Winchester, UK
Washington, USA

First published by Moon Books, 2013

Moon Books is an imprint of John Hunt Publishing Ltd., Laurel House, Station Approach, Alresford, Hants, SO24 9JH, UK
office1@jhpbooks.net
www.johnhuntpublishing.com
www.moon-books.net

For distributor details and how to order please visit the 'Ordering' section on our website.

Text copyright: Joanna van der Hoeven 2012

ISBN: 978 1 78099 390 4

A CIP catalogue record for this book is available from the British Library.

Design and cover photograph: Stuart Davies
www.stuartdaviesart.com

Printed and bound by CPI Group (UK) Ltd, Croydon, CRO 4YY, UK

CONTENTS

Acknowledgements	vi
Introduction	1

PART ONE – BACKGROUND

Chapter One – A Brief Overview of Zen	4
Chapter Two – The Zen Approach	14
Chapter Three – A Brief Overview of Druidry	23
Chapter Four – The Druid Approach	28

PART TWO – INTEGRATION

Chapter Five – Zen Druidry: Getting Started	36
Chapter Six – Meditation	42
Chapter Seven – Awakening to the Natural World	54
Chapter Eight – Mindfulness	60

Epilogue – Zen Druidry	63
Bibliography	65
Biography	66

Acknowledgments

I would like to thank my parents, who have always believed in and supported me.

I would also like to thank my teachers along the path, and in particular Emma Restall Orr, whose vision of Druidry inspired me to further my own.

Introduction

Zen Druidry – two words that you don't often hear together in the same sentence. The first brings to mind images of far off Eastern lands, Buddha and lotus flowers. The second evokes Celtic mysticism, mistletoe and sickles, long-bearded men in flowing robes. What could possibly happen when you bring the two together?

A practical, down-to-earth spirituality, philosophy and way of life.

The aim of this text is to show how Zen teachings and Druidry can combine to create a peaceful life path that is completely and utterly dedicated to the here and now, to the earth and her rhythms, and to the flow that is life itself. We will begin by looking at the history of both Zen and Druidry, where they share commonalities and where they differ. Then we will investigate the core tenets of each, again seeing the similarities and differences which make them both unique and yet related. Finally, we will show how the blending of the two creates a rich and fulfilling spirituality that anyone can follow if they so choose.

We will look at meditation, at the cycles of nature and of ourselves and at living in the present moment. Like the lotus flower, we will reveal the beauty that lies within each layer of perfection that is our self. Like the sickle, we will remove the dross and realise the potential that we all have if we have the courage to seek it out.

May we live our lives fully – not simply going with the flow, but by being the flow itself.

PART ONE

BACKGROUND

Chapter One

A Brief Overview of Zen

A Short History of Zen Buddhism

Zen doesn't have to relate to any religion at all. However, its origins are in the Eastern religion of Buddhism, and so we will start by looking at the history of Zen Buddhism.

The first thing that must be made clear is that the Buddha is not a god. Buddha was a man of the noble/warrior class in India, named Siddhartha Gautama. Siddhartha's father wanted him to become a great warrior leader, and not to pursue spiritual matters. He believed that if he could shield his son from any suffering, he would not need to turn to spirituality and therefore become a great warrior leader. Siddhartha was cut off from all contact with the outside world.

He grew up in the royal palace, never knowing or seeing anything of the outside world. He even married and had a child, still with no knowledge whatsoever of any external relationships. He never saw sickness in anything, be it person, plant or animal – these were carefully hidden from him. Flowers were not allowed to wither and die in the royal gardens, old age was hidden from him, death was a complete unknown to him. Eventually, he craved to know what life was like outside the palace, and snuck out in disguise for four nights with a single servant. What he learned shocked him to the core.

The first night he came across a very old man, and Siddhartha asked his servant why the man was so wrinkled and weary. His servant answered that the man was simply old, and that this is what happened to all men and women. On the second night, Siddhartha encountered someone who was lying sick in the road, and queried his servant on this. The servant replied that the man had an illness, and that all men and women were susceptible to disease. The third night, Siddhartha saw a dead body for the first time, and asked his servant why that person wasn't moving – was he asleep? The servant answered him no, and that the person was dead – all men and women would one day die. On the fourth and final night, Siddhartha saw a monk, travelling in search of truth, living in poverty but with a serene and fulfilled look on his face. Siddhartha again queried his servant, asking what was wrong with that man, as he had never known such a thing. The servant answered that the monk was searching for enlightenment, for the spiritual truth which would ease all suffering, and in doing so had forsaken all his material possessions.

Siddhartha was overwhelmed. Growing up as he had, with no knowledge of suffering, upon seeing the suffering in the real world it threw him into a spiritual turmoil. It was like standing under a waterfall, with all the pain of the human condition falling upon his head. He then vowed that he would find an answer to the suffering, and left the palace and his family to search out the truth.

Siddhartha's search lasted for six years. He began in poverty, and nearly starved to death. He studied many religions, with their adherents to the life of an ascetic, and discovered that was not the way to spiritual growth. He found that the path of moderation led to the most practical road in his quest to answer why all things suffered. Still he had not reached that answer, and one day, coming across a lovely bodhi tree (a fig tree) he sat down and vowed that he would not leave until he had gained the knowledge of why people suffered, the truth in all existence and the nature of the pure mind.

Siddhartha sat under the bodhi tree all night. The first thing he realised was the law of *karma*, of how all things are subject to a cause and an effect. The second thing he realised was how all things are related, and how there really was no separation. The third thing he realised was the true nature of suffering, and then how to alleviate suffering. As the sun rose he had attained enlightenment, reached nirvana and was a Buddha. He had discovered the *dharma*, or the truth of all things.

For forty more years up until his death he taught the dharma. He found and taught compassion for all things, and that all living things had a Buddha nature. Now the dharma is the teacher for Buddhism, flowing from teacher to student, from master to monk throughout the world.

Buddhism spread from India to China through a man called Bodhidharma. He went to China to teach the dharma, and went to meet with the emperor. The Emperor Wu of Liang was unimpressed, and turned him away. Bodhidharma then went to a monastery high in the mountains and found a cave where he sat and meditated, facing a wall, for nine years. He became the first of six patriarchs in Buddhism (those who have superior understanding and enlightenment).

Buddhism gained influences from Taoism in China, which greatly influences how we see modern Zen today. The principles of effortless effort, mindfulness, awareness and simplicity are all crucial to the Zen mindset. Buddhism then split into different sects, such as Ch'an (Chinese for Zen) which spread to Japan where it is called Zen (Zen means meditation in Japanese). In Japan, Zen gained further changes, with formalised and ritualised arts such as calligraphy, tea ceremonies, poetry and archery.

The Dharma Principles

The truth that Buddha realised was broken down and organized into many different parts – the Three Treasures, the Four Noble Truths, the Five Noble Precepts and the Eightfold Path. Many of these overlap with each other, to create a worldview that eases suffering and that holds ethical considerations high.

The Three Treasures

A very simple set of practices and beliefs in Buddhism are called the Three Treasures. It is in these treasures that everyone can find the path of least suffering.

Everyone has a Buddha nature
Follow the dharma
We are all one

Realising that everyone has a Buddha nature allows us to connect with others on a much deeper and more compassionate level. Compassion is key in Buddhism. There is a Zen Buddhist story of what one should do when one encounters Buddha on the road – kill him. Why? Because there is no Buddha outside ourselves. We must destroy this concept completely if we are to truly see reality for what it is. Seeing the Buddha nature in ourselves and thereby everyone engenders compassion. It can seem contradictory – Zen often is. It is often the crazy contradictions in Zen that allow the mind to be blown apart into thinking differently.

Following the dharma helps us to understand and reflect upon the ultimate truth. By following the Buddha's teachings we catch glimpses of enlightenment. As each day goes by with our understanding deepening of the dharma, those glimpses become longer and longer.

There is another Zen story about a fish, who kept asking the other fish, 'What is the ocean?' When he asked this question to a great master and enlightened fish, his only response was laughter. The fish is not separate from the ocean. The wave is a part of the ocean, even when it ceases to be a wave – it is still there, as the ocean. We are all like waves in the ocean.

The Four Noble Truths

The Four Nobles Truths help us to realise the problems we have in our life, and how to overcome them until we realise that there are no problems at all, simply life.

All living things experience suffering, or *dukkha*
Suffering is caused by desire, or attachment
Getting rid of desire shows us that we already have every-
thing we need
All things in moderation

Dukkha is an old Sanskrit word meaning suffering or dissatisfaction. It could be from a myriad things, such as losing your job,
to stubbing your toe on the bed. Sometimes we cannot yet name
our dukkha, but we have a sense of unease, or disease (dis-ease)
that won't go away. Every human being experiences this, as do all
living things. No one is perfect; we all deal with fear, anxiety,
pain, depression and disappointment. For the most part it seems
only humans make great drama about it – but we will cover that
later on in this book. Life is impermanent, and as such life is
imperfect and incomplete. It is only our reaction to this that
establishes a life lived with a greater or lesser amount of dukkha.

Desire is not only things we want, physically or mentally. We
may desire a person or an object – we may also have a desire that
life be different to what we think it should be. 'The grass is
always greener' syndrome is an element of desire. Desire can be
as simple wanting things to be other than they are. What we
desire is impermanent. By realising the impermanence in all
things, our desire, or attachment can grow less.

Eliminating desire leads to an elimination of suffering.
Constantly reaching for what we don't have, we often miss seeing
all the things we already do have. Ceasing to desire, or *nirodha*,
helps us to reach a state of *nirvana*, the place where desire cannot
exist. Nirvana is freedom from all the things that cause us pain or
suffering – worries, life problems, etc. Paradoxically, we should
never desire nirvana, for in doing so we will never achieve it.

By living in moderation, or following the Middle Way as
Buddha suggested, we eliminate desire, or at least ease it
somewhat. It is the middle ground between hedonism and

asceticism, where we find an 'easier' way to live – that is, to live with more ease and less struggle. The Middle Way is described in the Eightfold Path.

Five Noble Precepts

These are the key elements to living an ethical life. However, they are merely suggestions, not dogma. It is up to each individual to apply these to their own lives as best they can, and to continue to work on these with each and every day that passes. They are pretty self-explanatory:

The destruction of life causes suffering, so we learn compassion for all things and protect all that we can, whether it be the lives of people, plants or animals. We refuse to kill, or to condone any acts of killing.

Injustice exists in the world, and we vow to learn loving kindness so that we may work for the well-being of all, whether they be a person, a plant or an animal. We learn the value of sharing, of helping the community, and refuse to steal or harm in any way.

Sexual relationships must be treated with full respect, and we must not engage in any sexual misconduct, for this causes suffering. We must protect ourselves and others from sexual abuse and any other sexual misconduct.

Speech is a powerful thing – words have power. We must speak with attention to what we are saying, with loving kindness and working to resolve conflict. We must also listen with full attention to what others are saying.

Seek out the Middle Way – unmindful consumption causes suffering. We vow to create good physical health in ourselves and others by being mindful of what we eat, drink, and consume in our society to create the least amount of suffering.

The Eightfold Path

These contain the guidelines to easing the dukkha we all experience in our lives. It provides a strong platform from which to jump off and into a life of less suffering. It is the path to freeing one from attachments, and opening the mind to reality. The eightfold path is something to be lived, not merely contemplated.

Right view: through understanding that everyone suffers, and that life is impermanent, we begin to attain the wisdom to see the nature of all things. We see things as they really are.

Right intention: there is energy in our thoughts, and we must ensure that this energy is directed in a positive way. Our thoughts lead to our behaviour, and so with a compassionate mind towards all things, we refuse to engage in behaviour that cruel.

Right speech: words have power, words have weight. On the popular television show, *Northern Exposure*, this was stated with eloquence – words are heavy things – if birds talked, they could not fly. The importance of speech in our species is unquestionable. Buddha stated that we should not lie or attempt deceit, that we should not gossip or slander, that we should not hurt others with our words and that we should refrain from idle speech – speak less, think more.

Right action: this is also explained in the Five Noble Precepts. We should refuse to kill or act violently, we should not steal or be dishonest but live in a just way, we should abstain from sexual misconduct that harms others, we must talk sincerely and with honesty, and we should seek the Middle Way.

Right livelihood: in essence, this would be having an occupation that is in harmony with the Five Noble Precepts. It means having an occupation that is not harmful, such as the weapons trade. It suggests choosing a living that is just and compassionate.

Right effort: this means learning and living with a self-discipline that engenders compassion to all things. It is a conscious effort to live positively by preventing unwholesome states, to abandon any unwholesome states and to nurture and maintain wholesome states that have already arisen.

Right mindfulness: this is the controlled mental and physical faculty of being mindful all the time. We will look at mindfulness later, but in brief, it is being aware of things and seeing them for what they really are – your reactions to an event, your feelings, your environment. It is the recognition of all the other extraneous thought processes that occur after the initial impression of an event, such as judgement, anger, insolence and so on. The goal is to reach beyond these extraneous thoughts to a life of living in the pure moment with a pure mind.

Right concentration: often described as one-pointedness of mind, this is the development of the power of concentration by complete immersion in the present moment. It is achieved in Zen through meditation, where step by step we learn to deal with distractions and desires and achieve a fulfilled life thanks to our efforts in concentration.

Three Treasures, Four Noble Truths, Five Noble Precepts and the Eightfold Path – a lot to digest in one sitting! However, as stated previously, many of these overlap, and give a foundation for living a life without dukkha. It is all part of the dharma. They are not to be slavishly adhered to – they are not like the Christian commandments, with all their 'thou shalt not' – they are guidelines for a more wholesome life that only you can walk the path towards. There are several stories of Zen monks who followed all of these with strict adherence to the letter of the law, while missing the point entirely. Here are two of my favourites.

A monk and his student were standing at the crossing of a large stream. A beautiful woman stood nearby, upset that she could not cross as the current was too strong for her. Without a second thought, the monk picked her up and helped her across the stream, setting her down on the other side. As the monk and his student proceeded on towards their monastery, many hours later the student turned to the monk with a question.

'Master, why did you pick up that woman? Did you not know that in our monastery, it is forbidden to touch women? And she was beautiful!'

'Yes,' the monk said, 'but I put her down on the other side. I see you are still carrying her.'

A monk arrived late one evening at the monastery on a cold winter night. No one was around, so he built up a fire to warm himself. There was no wood available, and he was unable to chop any with the snowstorm that whirled outside the monastery windows. Looking around, he saw some wooden Buddha figures in alcoves. Picking up one of these, he set it alight and began to warm himself by the fire.

Another monk walked in, and saw what he was doing. 'You cannot do that!' he cried. 'That is a Buddha!'

'Do you mean that Buddha lives in this piece of wood?'

The other monk looked uncertain. 'No, that is impossible.'

'Excellent,' the monk said. 'May I have another Buddha for my fire?'

As you can see, Zen is a tradition that is steeped in common sense and the nonsensical at the same time – it is humorous and enlightening. All we can do is to strive without attachment to the ideals outlined in the above Dharma Principles to live a simpler, easier life with full awareness.

Chapter Two

The Zen Approach

The Nature of Suffering

We suffer because we become attached to things, people and ideas. We feel dissatisfied with our lives – we all have dukkha. With Zen, we learn to simply get on with our lives without the attachment, and therefore without the suffering. Zen is all about living.

What Zen teaches us is fine-tuned perception, so that we can see the attachments for what they really are. We love to attach to our feelings about situations, believing that they define us. For instance, we say we hate dusting the house. We tell everyone how much we hate it every time the subject of household chores comes up. When it is time to dust the house, we experience all the feelings we have attached to the chore. We spend our whole time hating it. Yet, what would happen if we simply got on with it and dusted the house, without all the feelings attached to it?

Instead of thinking, *I hate dusting*, we can be completely absorbed in the action of dusting. We pick up the cloth or feather-duster, feeling the texture, the weight. We move around the house, clearing it of the accumulated dust, really seeing it, smelling the house, paying close attention to each object. Any time a thought about how we hate it comes into our mind, we refocus our attention on what we are doing. We pick up the candlestick and dust it, then the place where it rests, with full attention. If we learn to concentrate fully on what we are doing, thoughts of hating dusting will never even enter our mind. This is also known as being mindful.

The moment we think about our suffering, we *are* suffering. If we don't think about it, the reality simply is. Physical pain is just pain, yet when we attach to our feelings of it, we find that it becomes intolerable, agonizing, unbearable. Have you ever stubbed your toe and really just felt the pain, instead of swearing, thinking about how much it hurt, how you will ever get your shoe on now, will the pain ever end? When we truly experience it, it simply is – and therefore life becomes easier than if we are still attaching to our pain.

We do not ignore our thoughts when they arise about a situation. To truly understand the nature of suffering we need to see these thoughts for what they are – thoughts – and *then* get on with it. Everything is impermanent anyway. What changes is that we realise our own impermanence alongside everything else. We hate change – as humans, we are constantly seeking security. If we change from the person who hates dusting to the person who dusts, is the change really so bad? It is our perception of change that needs to be addressed. Change is not a bad thing – it simply is.

Take for example the aging woman. In our culture, we do everything we can to maintain the look of youth, which we believe to be beautiful. The sight of that first wrinkle, that first gray hair, can cause great upset. We are no longer young. We are not who we want to be anymore. No one wants to be old, right? Our wants, our desires, are the root cause of suffering. If we no longer desire to look like we did when we were in our twenties, our attitude towards getting older shifts, and we simply accept it. Like the Christian saying:

> God grant me the serenity to accept the things I can't change, courage to change the things I can, and the wisdom to know the difference.

We shift our ideas about everything when we realise that every-thing changes. The true goal of Zen is to stop having attachments to everything and to simply experience. That would mean becoming completely enlightened and, while no one can be in that state all the time, there are a few out there who are close. This is true wisdom.

We use so much of our resources in our suffering. Life becomes much easier when we stop pouring energy into our thoughts about a situation. Instead of spending all morning thinking about our aging, going out to the shops and buying the latest wrinkle cream that won't work the miracles it claims – we come to the realisation that spending so much time and effort on that situation is a complete waste. So we have a wrinkle. We look in the mirror, shrug, and get on with brushing our teeth.

The main point to alleviate suffering is to realise that we are not in control. We like to think we are, because if someone is in charge, then things will head in the right direction.

Things will head in a direction whether or not you believe someone is in control.

The illusion of control is an intoxicating one. If we believe we are in full control of our lives, things will not go wrong. Can anyone state that, in their lives, nothing has ever gone wrong? We are not alone on this planet – we live alongside other people, other animals, the mountains, the wind and the rain. We have no control over these.

Giving up the illusion of control does not mean giving up responsibility, however. Responsibility is the ability to respond. If we see a cat lying hurt in the road, and we have the ability to respond, we should do so. We shouldn't walk away and say that we are not in control. We cannot use it as an excuse to avoid doing our duty according to the Five Noble Precepts. Remember compassion?

As an example, a friend of mine was having a team outing from work. His colleague had given people the wrong directions to point where they were to meet. If people had followed her directions, they would have ended up miles away. My friend decided to politely email her to let her know that at a critical junction in the directions, literally, they were to go left instead of right.

The response that he received was not at all what he was expecting. She insisted that her directions were right, as they came from her superior. She then insisted on getting upset about the whole affair, and speaking with anger towards my friend.

This upset my friend, as he was only trying to help everyone involved. He came home that night, still thinking about the situation which he had been going over and over again in his mind ever since it happened. When he told me about it, I could see the agitation in his body, hear it in his voice. He was still allowing this to upset him. Not only was someone rude towards him, but he felt that he had a responsibility to tell people the right directions. He was worried that if he did, this person would make the rest of his working life a living hell for him, and oppose him at every turn.

The first thing I reminded my friend of was the fact that we cannot control other people. There may have been many other factors that would attribute to her behaviour that we did not even consider – she may have had a bad day, her dog may have died, she may have just received a bollocking for an error in some other aspect of her work. At any rate, we should a) remind ourselves that we have no control; and b) have compassion for her. Though we may not know why she behaved the way she did, and we shouldn't agonise over the reasons why, for we may never truly know. We should still realise that she is a human being who is under the same suffering that we all experience.

Still my friend worried about it all night – should he or shouldn't he email everyone to let them know the right directions to the site? What would be at risk in his job if he did so? All I could do was encourage him to tell the truth, to email everyone with the right directions without any judgement of the previous directions, or mention of them at all if possible. It was his responsibility to ensure they all got there instead of wasting time and fuel driving all around the countryside. He could not control her reaction to the email, he simply had to get on with it. So he did.

What happened? They all got there, did a good job, and nothing was ever mentioned of it again.

The colleague did not make his work life difficult since then. My friend's job is no more or less than it was before. No one commented on the amendments to the directions even. They all just got on with it. The entire day, night and next morning, agonizing over the matter, had been a complete waste of time and energy.

Some people might think that the colleague should have at least apologised for her error. Perhaps I should state this one last time: we cannot control other people.

People may be rude to us. Buses may be late. People may not act as we would wish them to. And that is just the way life it. By not attaching to the feelings brought on by such situations, they simply happen. The bus is late. We will be late. That is all. Worry and stress won't make it come any faster.

The illusion of control is like the moonlight upon the water. We reach for the moon in the water, but we cannot grasp it. We may think that by giving up the illusion of control in our lives that we will fall behind in the dog-eat-dog world. However, it's not that hard to give up something you never had in the first place. Like the moon in the water, it is an illusion, not the reality.

Some people enjoy the drama that comes out of their suffering. This is a terrible attachment which is very hard to overcome because it gives us so much 'pleasure'. Yet when we realise that the pleasure too is an illusion, we can forgo it and simply live. Influenced by television, film and books, we act in a similar fashion to people in those tales – or how we think they would act. Life is not at all like EastEnders, and yet, how many people do you know who try to make their lives just like that particular show? I have known plenty in my brief time on this planet so far, for various reasons – boredom and low self-esteem ranking high. It is always from a sense of dissatisfaction, or dukkha, in their lives.

Why do we enjoy the drama in our lives so much? Various reasons – it gives us attention, it makes us feel important, it turns our attention away from other things. When something is happening *to* us, we enjoy the opportunity to extol upon this, whether the situation was a positive or negative one (yet, in reality, there are no positive or negative situations, merely situations).

The culprit for all personal dramas is the ego. Remove the ego, and all drama ceases to be.

Remove the ego? Who would I be then?

We are all under the false assumption that we are our egos. In effect, our egos consist of patterns of ingrained beliefs and behaviour. All of these can be changed. If all of these can be changed, then who are we? Is there a core person in the first instance, if we all have the ability to change? What would you say if I told you that you were not the centre of the universe? You would probably agree with me (I hope). What if I told you that you were not the centre of your own universe?

It is only our perception of ourselves as the centre of our little universe, with our dramas, that continue to lead to suffering and dissatisfaction in our lives. When we realise that, in fact, our own universe does not even exist, we can move away from both it and the drama that we create to sustain it – just think about all the energy that we pour into something that doesn't even exist. We cannot have our own universe, for we are sharing it all the time with everything on this planet, indeed in this universe. Uni – one. Not separate. When we realise that, our worldview shifts dramatically.

Not being the centre of our own universe means not attaching to every little or large thing that happens in our lives. If someone upsets me, who is the 'me' that they are upsetting? Why am I attaching to it, getting upset? For comfort from someone else, for attention, to be told that I am right and that they are a horrible person? Who is this person that is upsetting me? Who am I?

We don't have to attach to everything. Things will happen; we have no control over them. What we do have control over is our attachment to the reaction. Much like in nature – the daffodil rises early in January, and then dies from killing frosts in February. Does it get upset about it? Why do we let our human consciousness impede our lives so much in this way, when all of nature seems to cope without the drama? The daffodil will bloom again when it can – as simple as that.

When we realise that Buddha is in everyone, why be all dramatic about anything? As Charlotte Joko Beck stated, and titled a book – *Nothing Special*.

Living with this mindset, that life is nothing special, has, paradoxically, the effect of seeming to make everything special. Life becomes special, when we take our egos and the drama out of it, and see it for what it really is. It becomes *real*, as opposed to the imaginary world that we create to indulge our egos, our imaginary universe where we are the centre of existence. Which would you prefer to live in?

It's all very well to say that we shouldn't be dramatic about anything, but what about the really big tragedies our lives? What if we lose a child, or a parent dies? What if we lose everything in a house fire, or our plane is starting to go down? How do we deal with these crises? How do we get past the suffering that they can create?

Again, the suffering is not the situation, it is ourselves. It is our attachment to the situation that is causing the suffering. We react to everything all the time. The key in Zen is to perceive the reactions, and not follow through with the attachments that will lead to suffering.

Say a parent had just died. It is a sad time for you – you will never see them again. You will never hug them, or share a cup of tea, or chat about old times. You feel a great loss in your life. Your initial reaction is probably to cry. So cry.

I'm not saying that we shouldn't cry when we feel sad. In order to alleviate suffering, we must feel the feelings, we must perceive them and *then* move on. Like the stubbed toe, feel the pain and life eases sooner. Feel the sadness, express it literally or figuratively with your tears. However, don't attach to the sadness itself. Therein lies the danger. Experiencing is not attachment.

We can observe ourselves being sad. This won't make the sadness go away – that is our reaction. However, if we cling to the sadness for what it may be giving us, such as attention, then that is where we start to suffer. Some reactions last longer than others. Some emotions, like anger, may seem dangerous to experience. Yet it is the same as any emotion – we perceive it, we observe ourselves in it if we can, and we feel it. Acting on the emotion and feeling is where we tend to suffer. We should never act out in anger – not if we are following the road of compassion. We cannot lose ourselves in sadness, for we still have responsibilities. We feel them, and then we do what we can to alleviate suffering in our lives, and hopefully, the lives of others.

An interesting way to think of this would be to ask yourself the question, 'What would I do if I was to learn that I was going to die tomorrow?' Would you spend the whole time being angry at the fact that you don't have all that long to live? Would you spend that time being upset? Yes, your initial reaction would be shock, might be anger. Are you going to attach to the reaction, or are you going the make the most of the life that you have left?

You cannot ignore negative feelings. They simply won't go away until we experience them, without attachment. However, an equal danger lies in attaching to the positive feelings we have about our life experiences. Not everything is tragedy. We can have a wonderful day, and label it the best day – it is in that labelling where our suffering lies. If that was our best day, then all other days will fail in comparison.

So, how do we train ourselves to be able to perceive our

feelings and attachments to life experiences? In Zen, this is through meditation, which leads to a life of mindfulness.

Chapter Three

A Brief Overview of Druidry

Who Were the Celts?

To look at Druid history we must look to the history of the Celts, who they were and where they came from. There is a growing theory that the Celts had Indo-European roots dating back to around 4000 BCE, and migrated across Europe to finally settle in France, Britain and Ireland. (This is, to me, personally fascinating, as there is much in common between Buddhism, Hinduism and Celtic spirituality. Sharing a possible common starting point, where Buddhism and later Zen travel east, and Celtic spirituality and culture travel west, is indeed an interesting idea.) Traces of Celtic culture and history can be found throughout Europe, and indeed, for an in-depth musical investigation into the migration of the Celts, Canadian artist Loreena McKennitt has been exploring that theme widely in her songs, and is highly recommended. The large Celtic migration theory holds that the Celts, after arriving in Britain, came across the native British tribes, and either war or intermarriage ensued. There is another theory, however, that proposes the native tribes grew into bigger and more socially complex societies, into which some Continental Celts settled into, and from which the Celtic cultural and religious ideas spread *into* Europe rather than the other way around. This theory would hold that Druidry is the native religion of Britain. Both theories are interesting and as yet remain to be proven. However, the leaning is still towards larger migrations with waves of invasions into Britain.

It is difficult to interpret Druid history, as indeed like most history accounts, their story was written usually by the winners or in this case those hostile to the Celts in any sort of conflict. The ancient Celtic peoples followed an oral tradition and, as such, there are no written records in their own voice. Classical sources have written about the Celts, describing them as barbaric, or if feeling more generous, noble savages. They write of a hierarchy based upon the tribe's standing in war – essentially the strongest arm ruled the tribe and/or many other tribes. They also describe women warriors as equally fierce as their male counterparts.

The Druids are commonly believed to the priestly caste of the Celts, whose service was to the gods and to their people. The perception is that they held considerable sway in the sociological foundations of Celtic life, being the law-makers and king-makers. The Druids and indeed the Celts abided largely by the concept of giving their word – once given it was criminal and exceedingly distasteful to rescind. This links in with reputation – what was said of a person was of great import in Celtic society. A person's reputation was linked to their standing in society, where being strong, generous, brave, wise and just was the ideal. To be less than this could lead to expulsion.

In Ireland, there was already an established code, the rudiments of Brehon Law. This formed the basis of society, a native legal system that had developed before the arrival of Christianity (abolished in the 17th century thanks to Cromwell). Honour was all important to Brehon Law – your code of conduct was determined by it, and deviance from the law resulted in dishonour to clan, tribe and self. It contained the moral power of the people who followed it. Indeed, the sustainability and durability of Brehon Law is considerable, existing in Ireland since before the common era and living to see the reign of Queen Elizabeth I.

Brehon Law consisted of many aspects of everyday life, and also care and responsibility to one's tribe or community. Hospitals had already been running when Christianity arrived in Ireland. A form of welfare for those unable to work due to illness had been established. Medical practitioners had strict codes of conduct to follow. Honour prices had to be paid for transgressions against the law, such as a blood price for killing. The laws centre around the concepts of personal responsibility, the upholding of truth, service and simple common sense.

Classical and Other Sources

In 58 to 51 BCE, Julius Caesar led the Roman armies in the Gallic wars, conquering many Celtic kingdoms and chiefdoms in Gaul. Subsequently, the new rulers saw the threat that the Druid priest caste held, and took measures to remove them utterly from society. Emperor Tiberius banned Druidry, as well as those who read auguries and those who were healers (according to Pliny the Elder). Later accounts from other philosophers and academics relate to the law passed by Emperor Claudius that banned the once accepted form of following many gods of differing pantheons in Roman culture, claiming that one could not be a citizen of Rome and a Druid at the same time.

Caesar claimed in his texts that the Druids were one of two highly regarded classes in Celtic society, the other being equites, or horsemen. He writes that they were the power behind kings, and acted as judges to all. Caesar also writes of the Druid belief in reincarnation, and of the lores of astronomy, biology and theology that they upheld. He also points out human sacrifice within the Druid caste, often using criminals in their rituals, making much of the barbarism (from a culture that contained gladiatorial arenas). It must be said that modern historians widely regard Caesar's accounts as biased, greatly exaggerated and incredibly inaccurate, and that they were written in justification of a Celtic conquest.

Later sources mention Druids after the Christianisation of Britain and Ireland, written mostly by Christian monks – again hostile to the pagan Celts. The knowledge of Celtic culture and society by Christian monks is also questionable.

However, Druidry did not die out completely with the coming of the Christians. There was simply a merging of the two in many areas, an adoption of sacred times and places and placing Christian iconography and theology over the top of the earthier underlayers. Druid colleges that existed in Ireland and Britain transformed into Bardic colleges said to have existed up until the 17th century, and even possibly later. There is even the hypothesis that many Bardic colleges simply became Christian monasteries.

These Bardic colleges endeavoured to retain and preserve poetry, history, mythology and indeed genealogy as well as some of the 'magical' practices. In Ireland the Ogham alphabet, a 'magical' script was thought to have been invented as a secret language and often used as a divinatory tool. The art of divination seems to have been popular in ancient Druidry much as it is today. However, in the early 17th century the Flight of the Earls saw the patronage of these Bardic colleges fade, and eventually dissipate. There is a theory that 'hedge schools' were created through those who carried the teaching in the forms of music and poetry as wandering minstrels, and the word Bard was often used to describe this caste.

Druid Revival

The 18th century saw the birth of the Druid Revival, with the writings of John Aubrey, John Toland and William Stukeley making the most impact. Aubrey's theories and surveys on Stonehenge and Avebury awakened a romantic longing of connecting the sites with the ancient Druids. Toland was inspired by Aubrey and continued using Aubrey's theories as a platform. Stukeley too was interested in the archaeology of Avebury and Stonehenge. However, he had the bad timing of arriving a little too late, for the fashion of liking all things ancient and Druid had begun to change. He later became a clergyman, incorporating ideas of Druid groves and megaliths into his own personal life, and vicarage gardens!

Towards the latter end of the 18th century a second revival

was started in 1781 with Henry Hurle founding the Ancient Order of Druids in a London tavern. They incorporated Masonic ideas into their interpretation of Druidry, some of which are good, such as charitable work and community support, others absurd, such as gender exclusive male dominated gatherings.

Edward Williams, otherwise known as Iolo Morganwg, wrote many scripts that claimed to have been founded on ancient Druidry but which, in fact, had been mostly (if not entirely) forged by the man himself. While beautiful and inspiring, it was only 150 years after his death that the forgeries were found out.

The Celtic Twilight emerged in the late half of the 19th century with the poetic writings of Yeats leading the forefront. This brought forth a renewed interest in the study of all things Celtic, with translations of old texts and retelling of Celtic myths becoming popular through the works of people such as Lady Gregory, Alfred Nutt and John Rhys among others.

Druidry in the 20th century was further established by the likes of Ross Nichols and Lewis Spence. Spreading the interest to America in the early 1960s, it held for some an equally attractive mystical path to follow that differed from the growing interest in all things Eastern, such as Buddhism. From the 1980s onwards, prolific Druids such as Philip Carr-Gomm, Philip Shallcrass, and Emma Restall Orr made Druidry more accessible to everyone, bringing it up to date and begetting the tide of information and books that is now becoming more and more abundant on the subject of Druidry all over the globe.

Chapter Four

The Druid Approach

Awen and Relationship

Now that we've seen a brief history of Druidry, what does it mean to be a Druid today? What is the Druid approach to life and what encompasses the Druid's worldview?

A very important Welsh word often sums up the nature of Druidry – awen. Loosely translated, it means flowing spirit or inspiration. Awen is that, but also so much more. It is that spark that encourages the seed to sprout; the point where two souls meet and touch; the flash of insight gained from a single drop of dew. Awen is life itself, living in the beauty of its own truth.

It is through relationship, through connection, that awen is seen, experienced, tasted, felt. The Druid strives to maintain a connection throughout her life to the world around her, whether it be the wind and rain, the beetle and bee, the cat, lover or house guest. The Druid cannot be ignorant – we must *know* about something before we can connect to it. And so the Druid learns about where her water comes from, establishing a connection and relationship with it, rather than just letting it run from the tap, drinking it without thought. Through knowledge of the natural world (which includes the human worldview) she can carry the thread of connection with her in her daily life, making everything glow with the light that is awen. She takes time to be outdoors as much as she can, whether it is on her balcony in the urban jungle, or deep amidst the forests, high on the windswept moors or in a corner of a city park. Observing, listening, using all the senses she finds a deeper meaning, letting the awen flow through her veins, sink into her very bones, to better understand the world and her place within it.

There is no better teacher for Druidry than experience. Many,

many books have been written about Druidry in the past twenty years – yet all the book learning is for naught unless it is taken into a practical context. Druidry is not just in the head – it is a way of life. To understand the nature of life we must get our hands dirty, stand out in the rain, let the ocean waves crash against our legs at sunset. Awen cannot be read about – it must be experienced.

Many Druids, myself included, see the world from an animistic viewpoint. Everything within nature contains its own spirit, its own essence, that defines it from everything else around it. The soul song of the cat is expressed in its form, its behaviour, its life, which separates it from the dandelion. It is spirit that is manifest into physical form – though some forms we cannot see, for they may be on a microscopic level, or invisible like the wind – we can only see its effects on things. Yet still everything has its own spirit, its own song and its own path to true self expression. We often forget, as humans, that we are also of this same path.

As an animist, I see, honour and acknowledge that everything has a spirit, its own energy, its own sense of being, from beetle to bear, sequoia to sea, walnut to wind. That energy is what makes it what it is – I'm not a physicist by any means, and I barely understand physics, but even in 'inanimate' objects, particles can move at incredible speeds and energy gives the table I am writing on its solidity, for instance. All things hum, have a vibration, have an energy. My bathwater, treated as it is to remove bacteria, is still water – run off from the local reservoir, filled with the songs of rain and wind, of tears and urine, all the things that is 'water', since time began (if you believe in a linear version of time). The carrot from my garden is full of the energy of the earth, the sunlight and the water, packed with its own vitamins. My cats are fluid energy, predator and friend, singing their own songs of sleep and comfort, hunting and love, sunbeams and radiators. Everything is a collection of energy that forms a distinct pattern that we recognize as a chair, a computer, a loved one.

Seeing this energy, honouring it for what it is, it becomes less easy to dismiss things. The spider can no longer be crushed simply because it has found its way into our home. Household cleaning products that pollute our waterways are an abomination. Sweatshop factory clothing, clear-cut forests and unsustainable fishing become grievous crimes against the energy that is life. The food that we eat, what we consume, becomes sacred.

I recently read that people are trying to breed featherless chickens, to make it easier in the killing stages and getting them ready for production into meat. This to me is a crime against life, against the flow that is awen. It completely denies the nature of what a chicken is – it is no longer acknowledging a chicken as a chicken – it is merely a product, food, something to be consumed, a resource. It is viewed as *without spirit*. Like a forest or a field of wheat, it is just a crop – its value is in the return on investment. It denies the acknowledgement of wheat as wheat – a precious form of life that contains the seeds of the next generation much as we humans and every other thing does. Its potential no longer lies in life, but in financial gain. This is a singularly human trait – to observe and treat other living things as such.

In honouring the food that we eat, we re-establish that connection to the sacred, to life itself. Life has no opposite – it simply is. Most people think that the opposite of life is death. However, death is a singular event, thus making birth the opposite of death. Life has no opposite.

Growing as much of your own food as possible, being a part of the process, nurturing plants so that they may nourish you, and honouring the cycle, knowing that one day your own body will nourish the soil as you lie in the ground with nothing but a winding sheet, to slowly decay and feed the earth – this is all part of the process of honouring the sacredness in all things. It is part of the exchange that has nothing to do with money – it is the give and take, the relationship with the earth that all living things do. It's just us humans that screw that up, taking and taking more than we need, giving nothing in return. Seeing the sacredness, learning about the give and take, is what Druidry is all about – that is what any relationship is all about.

Druidry, perhaps more than any other strand of paganism in the wide weave of spiritual traditions, takes the environment into consideration on so many levels. Druidry – most commonly believed to be from the old Irish words *dru* and *wid* meaning 'oak knower', or even the Proto-European *deru* and *weid* 'oak-seeker' acknowledges this communion with nature in the very roots (pardon the pun) of the word.

So the Druid sacrifices ignorance about the natural world in order to establish a better relationship with it. It is not comfortable to be aware of how we are affecting the planet, of scrutinising our every action. This is where the sacrifice lies. With are constantly learning – no one is perfect. We use the tools we have to understand better how to live an honourable life – a life that honours everything within it and that sees the sacredness of all things. The Druid worldview brings with it a responsibility. No longer are we allowed to remain ignorant of the ways of our own environment. If we are to view it as a whole, then we must truly see every part that we also play within it. If the whole of nature has a spirit, then issues arise such as the taking of a life for food. Many within Druidry are vegetarian, if not vegan, and yet there are still many others who eat the flesh of an animal. Some do so claiming that ethically raised and slaughtered animals for food are perfectly acceptable to put on our plates. In my own vision of Druidry, the damage caused to the environment by the raising of animals for food does not allow that luxury of thinking. It takes much more energy and resources to raise animals for food than it does to plant in the same amount of land a sustainable, organic crop for food. In giving up animal meat we are caring more for our environment. At the same time, we sacrifice our ignorance of the weighty issues behind such matters to become fully aware. We must accept responsibility for our part.

The word environment has many meanings, however. Our immediate response to the word is the natural environment – nature. There are many other environments, however – little worlds created by human consciousness. We have our work environment, our home environment, our villages, communities and cities. There is the issue of human to human interaction as well as interaction with nature (though as humans are a part of nature, I realise that I am contradicting myself in some ways, but please bear with me). Our own sense of self, or self-awareness, creates a thorny path through which we must navigate carefully, in order not to injure ourselves or others. Unless one lives as a hermit, the Druid will have interaction with other human beings, some Druids, some not. As with the Druid relationship with nature, sensing the inherent consciousness within it, Druidry teaches us that same sense of consciousness in human interactions. I admit – it is a lot easier for some people to respect an old oak tree than most human beings, however to be fully aware of our relationship with others we must act with a certain sense of honour. The same sense of honour, in fact, that we give to nature. We may not like some human beings, much in the same way we may not like Brussels sprouts, but we still acknowledge and respect their place in the wider web.

So how do we relate to our environment? Again, this is where awen flows. To the Druid, inspiration lies all around us in the environment, whichever environment that may be. The word – inspiration – to inspire, to breathe in, reminds us of the active role we must take. Breathing in must, of course, be followed by breathing out – exhalation, reminding us that everything we do has consequences. Breathing is the most primitive and simplest way we relate to our environment, and the most effective way of remembering that we are a part of it. The air that we breathe is also the air our ancestors breathed 50, 100, 1,000 years ago. It is also the air that the willow, alder and yew trees exhaled 50, 100 or 1,000 years ago. The wasp breathes in the same air, the grasses and wildflowers exhaling into the deepening twilight.

We can relate to our environment by simply remembering how to breathe, what we breathe and how it is all connected. From that, we literally gain inspiration, as well as being inspired by it. The inspired Druid then exhales that inspiration, whether it be a song to the darkening skies before a thunderstorm, giving thanks before partaking in a meal, writing a symphony, throwing paint at a wall, doing charitable work for the community or dancing in the light of the moon. This establishes a communication between the Druid and the environment – speaking to each other, even if it is without words.

We relate to our environment though inspiration, and we are all related, as the Native American proverb says. It isn't simply communication with our environment, but a soul-deep sense of relativity – that we are all related. Recognising the relationship instils within us a sense of responsibility, of caring for the environment, whichever one it may be. If we see that we are related to the badgers living in the brownfield area soon to be redeveloped, then we also see that we must take action to ensure that they are safe. If we see that we are related to the food that we eat, we will ensure that we eat organically and, if possible, grow our own food as much as we can to develop that relationship even further. If we see that we are related to our neighbour next door, we are more likely to establish an honourable connection to them and the rest of the community. It creates a sense of caring for the environment and all within it, and it is no easy task.

The challenge that faces the Druid is to see clearly these relationships, and to act honourably in all regards. If this challenge is accepted, then the worldview is broadened considerably, as is the environment. The web of life will shimmer with inspiration along every thread.

PART TWO

INTEGRATION

Chapter Five

Zen Druidry – Getting Started

Integrating the Five Noble Precepts

We have looked at the history of both Zen and Druidry, and investigated the core tenets of each path. Now we will look at starting our first footsteps on the path of Zen Druidry, how to put what we have learned into practice and most importantly, how to make it practical!

Zen easily blends in with any form of religion, for it uses the gifts that you already possess, and emphasises the fact that you are perfect and perfectly who you are at this given moment in time – you can be no other. As we saw, Zen is about living in the here and now, this very present moment, which does not exclude any higher or other powers should this be your belief system. You could be a Zen Celtic Druid, a Zen Christian Druid, a Zen Animist Druid – the path is open to you and you only. Each path is different. You can make full use of the here and now and appreciate the natural world around you, its rhythms and sounds, smells and sights. The main point is that Zen does not contradict any religions – in fact, it adds new dimensions.

While most Zen practitioners may be Buddhists, this need not restrict you to the teachings of Buddha. If, like me, you find them beautiful and informative, feel free to incorporate them into your Druidry. There is no monopoly on wisdom. That wonderful saying about killing Buddha on the road when you meet him, for you are already perfect and Buddha cannot exist outside yourself, relates to Druidry on so many levels. Each living thing is simply living, doing the best they can at that particular moment. Realisation, perfection – it's already there within each living thing. Like a seed, you already carry that potential within your very self, and with the right nourishment and conditions, will blossom.

Zen, like Druidry, is in the living; in the doing. It's not an intellectual exercise. We all have jobs, families, obligations. Many of us have felt a call to enrich these with devotion to causes, gods or goddesses or art. There is nothing wrong with that – equally, there is nothing wrong with simply devoting oneself to living in the present moment with no external obligations. It is in the doing that we create the most change in our lives, not in the thinking, or praying, or anything similar.

Let's look at Buddha's Five Noble Precepts once more, and see how they relate to Druidry:

The destruction of life causes suffering, so we learn compassion for all things and protect all that we can, whether it be the lives of people, plants or animals. We refuse to kill, or to condone any acts of killing.

Many who follow the path of Druidry are vegetarian, seeing in our present day and culture no need to eat meat. The meat industry is so wasteful and so far from compassionate that it is abhorrent to many – any visit to a slaughterhouse will testify to this. While there are Druids who eat meat, many of them have raised the animals themselves and can vouch for their living conditions, ensuring that there is the least amount of suffering possible. More and more Druids have allotments, if there is not enough space in their own gardens, to grow and tend their own vegetables, and so to live with minimal impact upon our environment and our community.

There are also many Druids who do not condone any acts of war or violence. Druidry acknowledges the spirit in each and every thing – though many find it harder to see that in humanity than in the natural world around us. We close ourselves off to other humans in particular, for they appear to have much more power to hurt us than the tree at the bottom of the garden, or the grasshopper in the fields where we picnic. By seeing that there is no 'other', that we are all related and connected, any act of violence is also done to ourselves. Druidry is about opening to all forms of life and seeing the sacred in them all – yes, even in people you dislike. We never said Druidry was easy!

Injustice exists in the world, and we vow to learn loving kindness so that we may work for the well-being of all, whether they be a person, a plant or an animal. We learn the value of sharing, of helping the community, and refuse to steal or harm in any way.

We can't escape it – the world is unfair. It is unjust. Many people seek out justice to right this supposed wrong. However, this justice can often be at the expense of others. We involve other people in our 'fight' for justice. I'm not saying that we shouldn't upset the applecart every now and then, as long as it's our own cart and no one else's. What we can do instead is to cultivate the attitude of loving kindness, which in Buddhism is termed as *compassion*. In Druidry, I find that the word that most fits is *empathy*. Much as we find ways to relate to the bee, the ant, our grandfather, so too should we find ways to relate to everyone else in this world, whether or not they are being unjust towards us.

This is not pacifism. This is taking an active role in bridging that gap between 'us' and 'them'. We do not even have to *like* them, per se – we merely have to empathise with them. It brings a whole new world view into focus, where we are all walking towards a path that sees the relativity in all living things. In that relativity, we will only want to do good, to help others and the community. We realise that stealing is only stealing from ourselves. And so, while we may try to walk a mile in someone else's shoes, therefore ending up being a mile away and with their shoes – this doesn't quite work, though it is a funny thought! We can't escape injustice, since we cannot escape each other. We can only learn how to live fully with empathy for all living things. We'll have to give them back their shoes. They're our own shoes after all.

> Sexual relationships must be treated with full respect, and we must not engage in any sexual misconduct, for this causes suffering. We must protect ourselves and others from sexual abuse and any other sexual misconduct.

Many within Druidry see a sexual relationship as a very sacred thing. It is not to be misused or abused in any way. It is also a very natural thing and a very natural human tendency to want to express our feelings for others in a sexual manner. For us humans nowadays, sex is not about procreation so much as an expression of our feelings for one another. As such, we must be fully aware of each other's feelings, and not hurt each other in any form, sexual or otherwise. It is a paradigm – both sacred and mundane.

If we have cultivated an attitude of empathy, of loving kindness, then we fully allow others to choose a sexual path that causes no suffering to others. We must also protect others who are being abused by a sexual relationship – we cannot condone acts such as paedophilia. To each their own, as long as it harms none, whether that be a same sex relationship, a polyamorous relationship, or even a life of celibacy. We cannot discriminate towards others in this very personal sphere, so long as there is no suffering involved.

> Speech is a powerful thing – words have power. We must speak with attention to what we are saying, with loving kindness and working to resolve conflict. We must also listen with full attention to what others are saying.

We live in a verbal society. Words, whether spoken or written, have power – hence the phrase 'the power of the written word'. We attach truth to the written word in many cases. In Druidry, we recognise the gift of speech and the power that it has. In Zen, we have learned how we often simply react to a situation, rather than engaging fully with it. We must think before we speak, and be mindful of what we say. The Druids, as we have seen, were often the resolvers of conflict, and what better way than through the power of speech. Words cause conflict as often as they resolve it, and we must work towards the latter, for there is certainly enough of the former already!

In Druidry, we learn to listen – to the blackbirds singing at dusk, to the airplane overhead, to the bee buzzing amongst the daisies. So too should we learn to really listen to each other, and not merely hear each other. Too often we are 'listening' to someone while already forming a reply in our own heads before they have even finished speaking. Engaging fully with the moment means fully listening when someone is speaking.

Seek out the Middle Way – unmindful consumption causes suffering. We vow to create good physical health in ourselves and others by being mindful of what we eat, drink, and consume in our society to create the least amount of suffering.

This is a big one in Druidry – being mindful consumers. We see too many people, especially at Christmas time, engaging in a frenzied state of consumerism that doesn't really benefit anyone at all except the corporations that prey upon people by using the newly created meaning of that particular time of year. We become aware of who we are buying from, if we cannot make or grow it ourselves. We become aware of the practices involved in getting the product to our doorstep, every step of the way. We learn where our water comes from, how many food miles are in our bananas, whether they are organic or not. It is a cultivated awareness of every aspect of our life, in the same way that Zen is.

Druidry is pretty much the antithesis of being wasteful – for that is sacrilegious towards Druidry. Every disposable, non-organic diaper being thrown into a landfill is an affront to our world and to Druidry. It is not only the external world around us that affects our Druidry – it begins with our own physical body. Drinking, smoking, eating, taking drugs – these are not 'forbidden' in Druidry. It is in the excess of these things that causes suffering – alcoholism, cancer and emphysema, obesity and addiction. Seeking out a middle ground – avoiding asceticism, for that is simply the other end of the spectrum of excess – gives us the best platform to ground ourselves and live a fully integrated life.

These five precepts are an excellent starting point for merging Zen and Druidry. Yet we should remember that in Zen and in Druidry, our lives have already started, and we must live them fully! Right now!

Chapter Six

Meditation

Stopping to Get Started

Ironically, the best way to start on the path of Zen Druidry is to simply stop! We use meditation as a point that we can return to, again and again, to remind us of how to live in the present moment, fully and with awareness. We try to live as fully as we can all the time, but when we are just beginning on this path, taking time out to stop and simply be can result in a lifelong, lifestyle change. It really can affect how we live the rest of our lives – something so simple, yet so difficult.

Zen teaches us all about non-attachment. Druidry teaches us about relationship. It may sound contradictory, but both hold each other so deeply it is hard to extricate them. Non-attachment lets us get on with our lives, to live fully present in the moment, allowing us to see thoughts and actions and then let them go or act on them as we need to. Druidry, when applied with the mechanics of non-attachment, allows for a total immersion in the present moment, where true relationship can be obtained and where the awen flows as freely as it ever could. Like the blackbird singing at dusk, we are purely in the moment and by being in the moment, connected to everything and being true to our own nature.

Meditation helps us along the path to both non-attachment and connection. It stills the mind so that it can find the space to simple 'be'. Once we have achieved that state, we can come to know ourselves, our thought processes, the patterns we create in our head. Aware of these patterns, we can step outside them and see them for what they truly are. These patterns no longer impede us on our journey to true connection. We live with full awareness. It is not, as a lot of people believe, a way of emptying the mind and focusing on nothing – trying to focus on nothing is not, to me, living with awareness. It is seeing the obstacles that our minds create for us, which I term as 'mindtraps'.

Every day we are caught in mindtraps – little prisons of our own making. We are constantly hijacked by our thoughts and feelings, our attachments to them and our egos. We spin endlessly in circles until we fall down upon our backsides. The key to breaking free of these mindtraps is through meditation and observation.

When we meditate in the Zen style, or do *zazen* as it is called, we become aware of our bodies and our thoughts. We do not 'zone out', we are not 'away with the faeries' or pondering the mysteries of life – in zazen we focus on pure experience. This focus helps us in our lives when we are not in zazen. We are aware of how our bodies are feeling – whether our breath is shallow or deep, that twinge in our back, whether our facial muscles are tense or relaxed. We also turn that awareness to our surroundings, listening to the birdsong outside, or the traffic, feeling the breeze or the sunlight upon our shoulders. We are aware as much as is humanly possible of everything that is around us and within us. It is no easy task.

Our thoughts are constantly seeking to distract us from the comfortable reality that we have created. Even though this reality may be a false reality, it is still more comfortable than sitting, thinking about our headache or the plain 'boredom' of doing zazen. We daydream, we think through all our life's problems, we spin off in attempts to do anything but simply be in the moment, because we feel that we deserve otherwise. Remember that old saying, 'there is no time like the present'? Similarly, there is no experience other than this present moment – mayhap the best thing you could be doing is simply experiencing it right now.

We like to think. There is nothing wrong with thinking – we can solve problems, work out situations with a little forethought.

We plan – and again, there is nothing wrong with having life plans. It is our attachment to these plans that sets us off in another mindtrap – where if we don't achieve them our life can feel in ruins.

In zazen, we learn to observe. We sit, and we observe our bodies' attempts to defy our intention of just sitting still and being in the moment. Why do our bodies do this? Because they reflect our thoughts – our thoughts don't want to sit still – they want to run riot. In zazen, it is not so much controlling our thoughts, pushing them away or yelling at them to be quiet like unruly children – we observe the thoughts and gradually, through observing them, they become quieter. A new thought is a wonderful, shiny thing that we want to explore – whether it is a 'good' thought or a 'bad' thought. When we have observed that thought 100 times, it becomes a lot less interesting. This is what zazen is about.

If we think about what happened to us that upset us during the day, we can easily become lost in our emotional attachment to it. If we simply observe the thought – 'oh, I'm having a thought about this again' and then return our attention to simply sitting and being in the moment, then we are on the path to freedom from these mindtraps. Again, it is not easy – we may have to do this 10, 100 or 1,000 times before the thoughts settle down and we tire of them. With persistence, they will.

We must be careful, however, to simply observe, without 'being' the observer. If we become the observer, then we have created a separate entity that does not exist. If we are simply observing, then we are the pure moment. The past does not exist, neither does the future. It is only this moment, that is constantly changing, that exists. If thoughts about the past occur, you can observe them, but then ask yourself – 'where is the past right now?' It does not exist. When we worry about the future, we can ask ourselves 'where is the future right now?' It does not exist. Only this present, ever-changing moment exists.

I love to daydream – but not when I am in meditation. I set aside a time in the day to daydream, to come up with wonderful stories that may see the light of day in future novels or short stories. There is nothing wrong with imagination – it is a gift that should be used every day. We must learn, however, not to become lost in it, this imaginary world that might seem so much better than reality. Living in a pure moment does not leave us unthinking, mindless zombies. We are totally and completely present, truly living life to the fullest. That is the greatest gift.

So now it is time to break free of your mindtraps – by looking at what thoughts keep occurring, what keeps rising to the surface when you are being silent and still. By observing them you will notice them, notice the patterns that are created, the emotions and physical pain that may be attached to these thoughts and how they can so easily control your life. Once we see the existing pattern, we can weave our way into a new pattern, into a new cycle. Through zazen, we can take this into our everyday lives, and so, when someone upsets us, or hurts us, or brings us joy – we can see the pattern that is created and either choose to remain within it, or weave a new pattern upon the web of life. We can either live in this very moment, or stay within our mindtraps. The choice is ours.

Finding the Time

The first major concern with meditation is simply finding the time to meditate. A lot of people, Druid or otherwise, have said 'I simply do not have the time'. Yes, it can be difficult, say with a newborn baby – your life is dedicated to keeping your sanity, your child and your home together in some sort of functioning order. Could even five minutes a day make a difference?

You bet.

You're tired. You've had a bad day. The baby simply will not sleep – it has taken two hours to get her settled enough. You have maybe two to three hours until she wakes again for another feed.

Should you take this time to sleep, or get the laundry done? Of course. Could you spare five minutes beforehand to meditate? Probably – though if you simply cannot keep your eyes open, then sleep is most definitely the thing to do!

You've had a long day at work to get everything done before the holidays. You put your back out yesterday. Your mind is going at the speed of light, checking that everything you needed to get done has been done. Your spine is on fire – you can't even sit up anymore, you must lie down. Would watching a little television while lying on the couch put aside your thoughts for a couple of hours, and ease the pain in your back? Probably, but the thoughts will simply come back, most likely when you're in bed and trying to sleep. Could you meditate, at least for ten minutes beforehand? Of course! Even if you have to lie down to do it, you can always meditate.

Even in our fast-paced, hectic lifestyles, we can find the time to meditate. It may not be as often as we'd like, but we just simply have to get started, which is the hardest thing. It is so easy to say 'I'll start meditating tomorrow'. Tomorrow turns into next week, which turns into next month, which then turns into the next New Year's resolution, and so forth. Start now. However you are feeling, if you won't fall asleep, you can start right now.

How to Meditate

In Soto Zen, sitting meditation is at the heart of the practice, as opposed to the Rinzai tradition where koan meditation (illogical questions posed by master to student that are meant to free the mind – the sound of one hand clapping, for instance) is the preferred path. Some liken Soto Zen to sitting under a tree, waiting for the apple to fall, while Rinzai Zen shakes the branches a little. With walking meditations, in Soto it is slow and controlled whereas in Rinzai it is quick and controlled. Soto certainly feels quieter, softer, and more of a solitary path than Rinzai, where there is much more interaction between master and student, much more communication, activity and expression.

While I love the koan's ability to break the mind free of the shackles of traditional thinking, I prefer Soto Zen – for I believe that the best way to meditate is to create the quiet in our own minds through discipline as opposed to the distraction that is a koan, which will then lead to the quiet of knowing or not knowing the answer to the question posed. This is simply a personal preference – I would strongly suggest seeking out and learning more about both paths, Soto and Rinzai, to see which one appeals to you.

In Druidry, meditation is also very important, for by stilling the mind we can learn to reweave the threads that have become loose, that disconnect us from the rest of the world around us. We can examine our nemeton, that space of our edges, both mentally and physically – that area around ourselves that still holds our soul intention. Some people have called it the aura – it is our own personal sacred space, often the intimate space that we do not usually let strangers in. We can open and close our nemeton, blending them with others or closing them off, feeling edges merging or withdrawing through intimate interactions, whether it is with our lover, the beech tree in the garden, our co-worker. We use our nemeton to create a space where we can simply be ourselves, allowing our true soul expression. By stopping for a while, we can look at how and where we are, where our edges are, and re-establish that connection with life through simple sitting meditation, or walking meditation. The key is in the stopping.

Many Zen teachers are very strict about what position to sit in. Some believe that the lotus pose (sitting cross-legged, each foot on the opposite thigh) is the only pose for meditation, believing that this is how Buddha sat when he attained enlightenment. Well, I'm not Buddha, and my knees and hips haven't got that flexibility. Not many people in our Western culture have that flexibility – too many years of sitting in chairs and other activities have changed our bodies from the flexibility we once had as children. Some of that flexibility can be regained, through yoga, pilates, and other techniques, but for now I will only state one thing – be comfortable.

I tried for years to sit 'correctly' in a half-lotus pose (one foot on the opposite thigh). All I got from that was my circulation being cut off, pins and needles starting from my foot and then running up my leg, then full loss of feeling in one leg, switching over to the other as I switched my legs halfway through the meditation. I do not believe that cutting off circulation is in any way good for you, and so I have given this up completely. Even sitting in just a regular cross-legged pose, raised on a cushion so my knees are pushed down towards the ground (creating a very stable platform) my circulation is impaired, and so I have taken to sitting in a position that allows me to lean back a little – which requires a back support. I found, with that simple change of position, I could still sit cross-legged, the best position and most stable position if a chair is not possible, and maintain the blood flow through my body as it was intended to be. Whether I'm leaning slightly back on my sofa-bed or on a tree out on the heaths or in the forest, this seems to take the pressure off my legs. You must find a position that works for you, that doesn't cut off the circulation. You may have to sit in a chair, or even lie down – be aware that lying down can easily make you fall asleep. You can even make or purchase meditation benches – I have not tried these, but they do look interesting.

So, now that we are sitting comfortably (ensure that you are warm enough, that you have gone to the loo beforehand, that you aren't wearing any restrictive clothing) – now what do we do?

We just sit.

Yes, that's it. Just sitting – it can be and is remarkably interesting. Really.

When we have stilled our bodies, our minds hopefully will still also. Remember that saying, *free your mind and your ass will follow*? What I am suggesting is to keep still on your butt, therefore stilling your mind. Starting with ten minutes a day, then in a couple of weeks twenty, then thirty, building up to an hour – we learn to make the time and space that we need to be still.

So how on earth do we keep still? Discipline, discipline, discipline. It's become a rather 'bad' word in our society today, instilling images of rigid conservative behaviour. What we must realise is that though we cannot control others, we can learn to control ourselves, and thereby act more honourably to the world around us, simply by being aware of ourselves. So we must learn to keep still, in order to attain that stillness within that will then allow us to hear the songs of everything around us fully. Our minds are chattering to us all the time – how on earth are we supposed to hear anything other than ourselves? Here, meditation is the key.

It helps to begin with a focus. When beginning on the path of meditation, whether with eyes open or closed, breathing is usually the first thing that we relearn how to do. We learn to become aware of our breath once again, really feeling our lungs expanding and contracting, the coolness of the air, or the damp, the moisture, the dryness of it. We feel it going through our noses (I prefer to breathe through my nose in meditation – for me it is quieter and I think it is better to use our natural filters in our noses), we feel it tingling past our nostril hairs, down into our throat and lungs, feeling the expansion of our chest, the contraction of our upper back, our diaphragm pushed down. Equally, we acknowledge the exhalation – the warm air again travelling from our lungs and throat out our noses, our diaphragms moving upwards again, the expansion of the upper back. We may even count our breaths, in sets of three, or nine, or ten. Yet again, I simply prefer to focus on the breath, for I believe that counting is still engaging our brains into repetitive patterns that we are trying to avoid – we are still hearing that voice in our head counting, which makes it more difficult to hear anything else.

The first few breaths we take in meditation are glorious – we are fully aware of the process, feeling it through our bodies, really engaging with what was once an automatic response to our need for air. But the novelty wears off so very soon, with our minds so accustomed to distraction. Living with television and the internet, radio and other media, we are constantly absorbing information, doing multiple things at once, dropping one thing and heading over to the next stimulus. In meditation, we learn to be without the man-made stimulus that we have grown so accustomed to. It's bloody hard.

And so, our minds instantly wander, reliving what happened in the office today, what our lover said to us this morning, what we are going to have for dinner. Appointments, engagements, things to do – all these suddenly surface and before we know it, we've lost our focus on our breath. So we return our focus as soon as we realise we have lost it. This happens, again and again. Trust me. It may happen ten times in one session, it may happen one hundred times, but it usually will happen.

This is where discipline kicks in. We are not, as stated before, trying to empty our minds. For now, we are simply trying to find a focus which will lead towards a path of stillness. We are wanting to open the door to awareness, but first we must focus our intent, grab hold of the doorknob, and turn it before we can enter into the next phase.

From there, we become aware of what is going on around us – shifting the focus slightly from our breath to our external world. We listen to the blackbird singing outside our window – but we listen without judgement, without thought – we simply hear it, without thinking about how beautiful it is, whether it will nest in our hedges, what time it is as he usually sings at dusk. Is it nearly dusk? Damn, we're supposed to be going out tonight – you see where I'm going with this! We hear the traffic passing by, the cooing of the doves, the sounds of children playing, the hum of our refrigerator, the central heating coming on. We listen without thought, without judgement. If we are outside, we can also feel the sunlight on our face and shoulders, or the wind in our hair, the raindrop on our skin, without attaching to it.

Like I said before, just sitting can be remarkably interesting.

We are not 'away with the faeries' in meditation – we are truly and more aware of what is going on around us than most people at that moment. We are also aware of our own bodies – any tightness, any pains, where we are relaxed and where we are tense. We can adjust our bodies, again without attachment, releasing tension and then moving on to full awareness of everything.

This first phase of meditation is exceedingly important. Once we have attained a modicum of discipline, we can then open ourselves up to what is going on around us without instantly jumping into thoughts about everything we see, hear or smell. We have already modified our behavioural patterns into something much simpler, much more integrated with the world around us.

The next phase is to allow the thoughts to rise, releasing the focus on our breath and our environment. We do not become absorbed in these thoughts, however. We let them bubble up, notice them, and then *without paying any more attention to them let them go*. This is the key – like an angry child with a temper tantrum, the more attention we give to our thoughts, the louder they will become, until they have completely absorbed us into their own little world. We must realise that their little world doesn't even exist – we must learn to stop living inside our heads.

Some of the thoughts that arise might be full of emotion, leading us to joyous recollections or into the pits of despair. Again, we must simply see the thoughts that arise in these first stages of meditation, and later find the space to deal with them should they need to be dealt with. The idea of mindfulness is not to push aside the feelings, not to suppress them in any way. You truly have to feel them – and with such feelings like rage, it can be difficult. But it is possible to feel these emotions without acting upon them. It's why I haven't murdered anyone – and I hope I never will! Because we live in honourable relationship to the world, we know that to act on certain feelings is morally unethical. We can still feel them, acknowledge them – hell, we're only monkeys with car keys after all. We honour the feelings of our own human nature, dance with them, surrender into their flow for a time, but never ever submit, for to do so could quite possibly mean our death, or the death and harm of others.

We can then set aside the time to deal with these feelings – by acknowledging the feelings through meditation, truly finding a space to feel them, we can then let them pass so that we may experience other feelings with the gift that is this life. Attachment to the emotion is what causes so much trouble. So, if I am filled with rage, I will sit with that emotion, rocking back and forth with the terrible power that it brings, possibly weeping, feeling it course through my body and my soul, my nemeton filled with it. At the moment when I first felt that rage, possibly earlier that day, or in that week, it was most likely not a good time to express it if I wanted to maintain an honourable and peaceful relationship with the world around me. And when the power from the emotion subsides, for it always does with the ebbs and flows of the tides of emotion, then we can look back at our experience of rage, and say – there. It is done. I had my reaction to the event. Anything more is attachment to it, for whatever reason it may bring us – sympathy, attention, apathy, whatever. The same can be said for joyous emotions as well. With Zen, it is the attachment to the emotion that causes suffering, not the emotion itself. With Druidry, we allow ourselves the time to experience the wild side of our natural emotions, the release that is integral to living.

We must express our emotions. But we must do so honourably. It is not honourable for me to scream at someone at work. If I am truly connected to all things, to this world right now, then to scream at someone is to scream at myself. What would be the point? I must take a step back, look at myself, look at them, and find the balance point where our two souls might meet again, and if that is not possible, then, with respect, walk away. So that life may be truly lived. The raw, tooth and claw emotions are what we all feel – we can't suppress them without damage to ourselves, but we can find the right space and time to experience them, to open our nemeton and let it flow. Inhale, exhale, breathe...

Once we have learned to see our thoughts for what they are, once we learn to deal with our emotions in an honourable way, we are well on the path to living outside our minds, and fully interacting with the world around us in total awareness.

Chapter Seven

Awakening to the Natural World

Attunement

At many Zen centres, meditation, which is at the heart of Zen, is often practised indoors, as it is the most accessible and easily maintained quiet, communal space with the least amount of distractions for the meditator who is beginning on the path. I encourage people to practise indoors at first, where they won't be distracted by noises and inclement weather. Once we have learned to sit still in meditation for at least twenty minutes, if not half an hour to an hour, we can then take our meditation outside and integrate it with the natural world around us. From there, we can learn to live with full awareness of our natural environment, whether it be indoors or outdoors, every day and every night.

Attuning with the cycles of the seasons is at the very core of Druidry – it is about learning what is happening in our current environment, the constant flux and change of time, the seasons and the weather. Often here in the UK we can have four seasons in one day – a bit of a challenge to attune to! Still, we learn to identify certain points in the cycle, markers if you will, that guide us on our path of integration and relationship.

There are many natural markers that we can use to help us attune to nature – the cycles of the sun and moon, the tides if you live by the ocean, the seasons. Even in an urban environment, most of these cycles can be followed.

In Druidry, there are eight seasonal festivals which occur roughly every one and a half months throughout the year. These follow the cycle of the sun and the seasons. There are many books already written on Druidry which go into details on the seasonal festivals (included in the bibliography) so we will not cover the same ground here, but instead give a brief overview.

Incorporating Zen principles and attitudes into these festivals can make them even more special and meaningful, personal and poignant. Combining the festivals to an attribute of the Eightfold Path can be even more enlightening, and help to alleviate dukkha, living a life of less suffering.

The Eight Festivals of the Year

We begin in the dark of winter, at the Winter Solstice, which occurs between 20 - 22 December. This is the longest night of the year, and the balance is about to tip over to lengthening days with more sunlight. In Britain, where the days can be terribly short, especially on dark, overcast wintry days, this shift towards the light half of the year is very remarkable and special for some people – not least those who suffer from Seasonal Affective Disorder. It is a time of darkness, of quiet contemplation and of family. Bringing sprigs of greenery into the home to decorate the hearth and integrate the natural world with the inner sanctums, and the giving of gifts that is now traditional at this time of year, strengthens the family and community bonds. It is a time for rest, as the earth lies dormant, seeds waiting below ground for the return of the sun as the cold winds blow. This is the perfect time to contemplate Right Mindfulness – understanding your reactions to events, places, people. Through meditation at this darkest time of the year we have the perfect opportunity to look inwards, getting to our core and learning to truly live instead of simply reacting to the world around us. Exploring thought patterns and bodily reactions through this deep, incisive investigation, we can really come to know who we are and what our place in the world is.

At Imbolc we welcome the lengthening days and the first of the flowers, with the snowdrops coming into season. For those that celebrate by the calendar, Imbolc occurs on the 2nd February. I prefer to celebrate when the snowdrops are out, as I find this more in tune with the seasons. This could happen anytime from beginning of January to as late as March, depending on the winter. Imbolc is also the time when the sheep begin to produce milk – ewe's milk, which is where we get the name Imbolc from. For our ancestors, this was a celebratory time, when cheeses and butter could once again be made to replenish the winter stores. Again, the milking time can occur anytime in February onwards – it's always a joy to watch the fields and wait to see the new lambs scampering, flipping their ridiculous tails! This is a time for preparing the seeds of what we wish to achieve in the coming year, dreamt up over the long winter nights, but not yet ready to plant – we must still keep these dreams safe. With Zen, we can apply Right Concentration to this time of year, and focus on total immersion in the present moment. It requires effort and discipline to concentrate on the present moment, but as the tides of light are growing we can find the inspiration to do so all around us, from meditating with a path of snowdrops to watching the sunset every day a little further along the horizon.

The Spring Equinox is one of two very special times of balance and of change. It is a liminal time, a time that hovers between two realities, waiting to see what will befall. The tides are changing over, and at this time the day prevails over the night, when the days become longer than the nights, the sun rising and setting further apart along the horizon. It is a time of change – we can stand on the precipice, waiting to see what happens, until we either lose our balance, are pushed or jump headlong into our lives. The greening is just about to happen – nature is about to explode in riotous growth, blossoms beginning to appear. It is also the hungry time of year for our ancestors – when the winter stores were running very thin, but the crops in the fields were not yet ready – food was scarce, and spring claimed more deaths than winter ever could for those who lived off the land. It is a time for Right Intention – the year lies before us with the promise of spring, and we must remember that there is energy in our thoughts, and that this energy is directed in a positive way.

Remembering that our thoughts lead to our behaviour, we find compassion, and refuse to engage in behaviour that can be cruel. At this changeable time, we determine the course of the light half of the year inasmuch as we can in our own lives, and sow the seeds that will bring about change.

At Beltane, or May Day, on the 1st May all life rejoices in fertility. The hawthorn, or May bush, is usually in bloom at this time of year, and in nature we see the beautiful mating game, the dance and the courtship that will hopefully produce something wonderful later in the year. The sap is rising in the trees and in our own blood, and we feel rejuvenated, alive in beauteous glory that the coming summer will bring. It is a time of expression – a reminder of the cycle, in that every inhale must have an exhale, and so we release into the tides of summer, riding the waves of energy that pulsate through the land. At this time of year we are all young, no matter what our years – and it is important to have the Right View. Living in the moment we see that life is imper-manent, though we may feel immortal at this time of year. With the knowledge of the impermanence of life, of its continual change, we come to an understanding that everyone suffers, and we begin to attain the wisdom to see the nature of all things. This is the time to open up your eyes, to see things as they really are.

At Midsummer, or the Summer Solstice, we revel in the time of longest light – the days seem to linger forever, the twilight hours bringing cool release from the heat of the day, and the very short nights give way to early dawn. The sun is at its peak, and so too can we feel the same way at this time of year. Honouring the cycle of the sun is important in Druidry, and reflecting the times and tides back so that we can better attune ourselves to the world around us is all important. This is also a challenging time, for those sensitive to the light, or heat – it is a time for the making or breaking of a soul, much like the Winter Solstice. This is the time for Right Action, for at the height of our powers we should act responsibly. We cannot act out of self interest alone, for we are not alone in this world. It is a time of sincerity and honesty, and with that we strengthen ourselves for the dark half of the year, just around the corner. The tides are constantly changing, and though we may be at our height, our fall is yet to come.

At the beginning of August is Lughnasad, or Lammas, the celebration of the cutting of the first crop. It is a time to see the product of our work since the long dreaming and introspection of winter. If we have worked hard, and external factors beyond our control (and nothing is ever under our total control) have been beneficial to our plans, then what we have sown in the spring should now start to come to fruition. The flowers are out in full force, the trees swaying in the breeze, and the long dog days of August lie ahead. There is no time to stop, we must still keep at our work for our harvest to be fruitful. It is a time for exchange and trade as well – for at this time our ancestors gathered to celebrate the first harvest with festivals honouring not only the time of year, but also to honour community and family. Love that bloomed in the spring came to marriage in August, vows were exchanged, goods and labour agreed upon. The time for Right Speech falls into this tide neatly – words have power, words have weight. Our words, reflections and projections of our thoughts, should not hurt others, but serve to strengthen our compassion and intentions for the good of all.

The Autumn Equinox brings us again to that point of balance where we wait upon the edge for the tide to turn to the dark half of the year, where the nights become longer than the days. The leaves are beginning to change, the nights are chill and the best of the flowers have gone. Nature is slowly winding down, animals are beginning their migrations. The tractors and combine harvesters are out in full force, gathering the crops of onions, turnips and corn. The deer are beginning to come together in larger herds for the winter – all are making preparations for the colder months. Our ancestors did as much as they could to prepare for the winter, and so too should we – even in our much easier, softer existence. This is the time for Right Livelihood, ensuring that what we do for a living is compassionate, and does not abuse others or the environment. Our ancestors needed to come together at this time of year to ensure they made it through the dark days of winter, so too must we come together to see that the impact that we make upon this planet, our home, is for the benefit of all, and not just the few, or our own selves. We must share in the bounty that we have harvested.

Samhain, Hallowe'en, All Soul's Night – for many pagans this is the ending of one year and the beginning of another. It is often seen as the third and final harvest – the last of the apples, the cattle prepared for winter, the grain stored properly. It is also a time when it is said that the veil between the worlds is thin, and the realms of the living and the dead are laid bare to each other. We are approaching the darkest time of the year, and the killing frosts and snows await just around the corner. It is a time of letting go, of releasing into the dark half of the year, and getting rid of the dross in our lives, so that we do not have to carry them with us through the long winter nights. It is a time of Right Effort, where with self discipline we learn compassion and empathy. We consciously make the effort to live better, meaningful lives and let go of what holds us back – our fears and worries, our anger and hatred. We also nurture the beneficial and the good that we have in our lives with just as much effort, ensuring that they are well kept for our plans to come at the Winter Solstice. So the cycle continues.

Chapter Eight

Mindfulness

Living in the Moment

We are classed as homo sapiens – humans that are aware. Yet how aware are we in and of our lives? The key to integrating Zen and Druidry lies in the path mindfulness – living with full attention. This is what makes Zen so wonderful, and so applicable to our lives and our spirituality, whatever they may be. In Sanskrit, mindfulness is *smriti*, which also means recollection, the state of being alert and also retention. It is a word that describes a myriad functions with simplicity – it *is* Zen, in a word.

The doors to mindfulness open with meditation, as we bring our awareness to our bodies and our environment through stillness. However, mindfulness need not stop there – it must be brought into our lives as a whole in order for it to function properly, much as our Druidry. When we bring mindfulness to washing the dishes, to setting up a ritual space, to petting the cat – this is where we truly live our spirituality. It is also releasing from the notion of there being a separate self, a release of habits and also judgements. It is release from our subjective self, with its endless opinions. As the Zen saying goes, 'Do not seek truth, only cease to cherish opinions'.

Druidry is all about relationship with the natural world. If we are truly mindful, that relationship will have so much more meaning. We really begin to understand that we are part of an ever-changing world, in a constant flux, with no single moment defining who or what we are – merely an endless series of moments which we all share on our journey through life. Mary Jaksch said, 'When we are mindful, we are available for life, and aren't trapped in our own little world' (www.goodlifezen.com). It is taking relationship and bringing it to the highest level possible of being fully present.

Bringing mindfulness into Druidry completely changed the way I practised my beliefs. I realised that sometimes I simply went through the motions in ritual, which is disrespectful in the least, and also a complete waste of time in other regards, for why else do ritual but to take the time to stop, pause and honour the moment? If you're not truly there for that moment, you might as well have not even bothered...

And so, mindfulness in ritual is exceedingly important. From the moment the ritual begins, we can truly be there, delving fully into the moment. Whether it is indoors or outdoors, we can feel the air on our skin, really hear the sounds around us, feel our breath. If we are with others, we can feel their energy, sense where their nemeton connects with ours and with the world at large. We can become aware on so many levels that it brings a richness and vitality that we never thought to achieve. Words spoken in ritual take on new meaning and power, as we feel our breath, our vocal chords thrumming with words or song. Physical actions have an intensity of purpose never before imagined – from the single act of striking a match and saying a prayer to the spirit of fire, to dancing a whirling dervish around the living room.

In Zen this is sometimes called 'before thinking', or 'true mind'. Relating this to Druidry, it is about being the most natural you can be, in relation to everything around you. It is dropping all the nonsense that clutters the mind and being free from the traps that the mind sets to keep it running around in circles, and thereby distracting yourself from true experience. The more you meditate in stillness, coming to understand the mind, the easier it will be to find the nature of your true mind.

It is then a simple step to bring that true mind out into the world, as we see the leaves turn in the autumn, or hear the fox barking at dusk. We become immersed in the present moment (not only in ritual, but in each moment of our life) and nothing slips past unnoticed. It is a celebration of life in each and every second. Not only can we carry our mindfulness into our daily lives, but we can also carry our Druidry with us, wherever we go or whatever we are doing.

There is an Irish triad, that states:

Three virtues of Wisdom: to be aware of all things, to endure all things, to be removed from all things.

This relates beautifully to Zen Druidry – awareness, perseverance and detachment from the unnecessary. We are aware of our world through being mindful, we are steadfast in our journey to be mindful, and we let go of all that holds us back in our own worlds to better experience the reality of this beautiful life that we all share.

We hear and attune, fully experiencing the earth and her rhythms. We dedicate ourselves to further understanding these, through relationship and empathy, compassion and determination. We become aware of nature's cycles and our own cycles, encouraging those seeds that will nourish us to grow, and letting go of all that holds us back. It is living with the courage to be fully present, whatever the reality. It is connecting to ourselves, our gods, our world around us, with dedication and determination.

It is letting go into the flow of awen, of satori, of truly being.

Epilogue

Zen Druidry

Taking both Zen and Druidry and embracing them into your life can be a wonderful and ongoing process of discovery, not only of the self but of the entire world around you. Looking at ourselves and at the natural world around us, we realise that everything is in constant change and flux – like waves on the ocean, they are all part of one thing that is made up of everything. Even after the wave has crashed upon the shore, the ocean is still there, the wave is still there – it has merely changed its form.

'Be a light unto thyself,' said Buddha. You don't have to embrace Buddhism to understand Zen. As I stated previously, there is no monopoly on wisdom. Only we can unlock the doors that keep us restrained in our minds and in our non-existent worlds – the worlds that are not reality. We are simply too caught up in ourselves to see reality for what it is, unfolding beautifully around us with each and every second. Our time is limited on this earth, in this incarnation – why waste it? By being mindful, by knowing ourselves, we can truly live.

We must acknowledge the world around us, and stop living in our little bubbles. With respect, honour and integrity we learn to live with ourselves and each other and, when the time to release is upon us, like the wave crashing upon the shore, we will do so with abandon, letting go when the time has come for it all to end.

Without getting caught up in ourselves, we can fully live and love with awareness. Feeling the earth beneath your feet, you walk up to the apple tree, inhaling the autumn air, feeling the caress of the wind in your hair and upon your neck. Feeling each and every muscle, acknowledging the intent formed by the thought in your mind, you reach out to pluck an apple from the tree, and give your heartfelt thanks in return for its bounty. You step back, knowing that all around you are millions upon millions of stories all happening at the same time, not merely your own. You feel the apple in your palm, inhale its scent and then, with total focus, take a bite, feeling teeth pierce the skin into the flesh, truly tasting every last morsel in your mouth even as the juice drips down your chin. And around you the world turns, and you turn within it, with compassion and empathy, alive, aware, awake.

Bibliography

Adamson, E. & McClain, G. (2001) *The Complete Idiot's Guide to Zen Living* Alpha

Allen, R. (2002) *Zen Questions* London: MQ Publications Limited

Beck, C. J. (1997) *Everyday Zen* London: Thorsons

Beck, C. J. (1995) *Nothing Special: Living Zen* New York: Harper Collins

Hutton, R. (2011) *Blood & Mistletoe: The History of the Druids of Britain* Yale University Press

Hutton, R. (1995) *The Triumph of the Moon: A History of Modern Pagan Witchcraft* Oxford Paperbacks

Restall Orr, E. (2004) *Living Druidry: Magical Spirituality for the Wild Soul* London: Piatkus Books Ltd

Restall Orr, E. (2007) *Living With Honour: A Pagan Ethics* O Books

Restall Orr, E. (2000) *Ritual: A Guide to Life, Love & Inspiration* London: Thorsons

Internet Resources

The British Druid Order www.druidry.co.uk

The Druid Network druidnetwork.org

The Order of Bards, Ovates and Druids www.druidry.org

Zen Buddhism www.sacred-texts.com/bud/zen/index.htm

Zen Guide www.zenguide.com

Joanna's Blog www.downtheforestpath.wordpress.com

Joanna's Website www.joannavanderhoeven.com

Biography

Joanna van der Hoeven was born in Quebec, Canada. She moved to the UK in 1998, where she now lives with her husband in a small village near the coast of the North Sea.

Joanna is a former Trustee of The Druid Network. She has studied with Emma Restall Orr and the Order of Bards, Ovates and Druids. She has a BA Hons English Language and Literature degree. She is regularly involved with charities and working for her local community. For more information about the author, please visit www.joannavanderhoeven.com

Other Books by the Author

Pagan Portals - Dancing with Nemetona: A Druid's exploration of sanctuary and sacred space
An in-depth look at a little-known goddess that can help bring peace and sanctuary into your life.

Nemetona is an ancient goddess whose song is heard deep within the earth and also deep within the human soul. She is the Lady of Sanctuary, of Sacred Groves and Sacred Spaces. She is present within the home, within our sacred groves, our rites and in all the spaces that we hold dear to our hearts. She also lies within, allowing us to feel at ease wherever we are in the world through her energy of holding, of transformation. She holds the stillness and quiet of a perfect day; she is the stillness at the end of it, when the blackbird sings to the dusk. She is the energy of sacred space, where we can stretch out our souls and truly come alive, to be who we wish to be, filled with the magic of potential.Rediscover this ancient goddess and dance with a Druid to the songs of Nemetona. Learn how to reconnect with this goddess in ritual, songs, chants, meditation and more.

Paperback 9781782793274
Ebook 9781782793267

Moon Books invites you to begin or deepen your encounter with Paganism, in all its rich, creative, flourishing forms.